2ND EDITION

CHRISTMAS CLASSICS FOR ACOUSTIC GUITAR

ISBN: 978-1-5400-2951-5

Visit Hal Leonard Online at
www.halleonard.com

Contact Us:
Hal Leonard
7777 West Bluemound Road
Milwaukee, WI 53213
Email: info@halleonard.com

In Europe contact:
Hal Leonard Europe Limited
Distribution Centre, Newmarket Road
Bury St Edmunds, Suffolk, IP33 3YB
Email: info@halleonardeurope.com

In Australia contact:
Hal Leonard Australia Pty. Ltd.
4 Lentara Court
Cheltenham, Victoria, 3192 Australia
Email: info@halleonard.com.au

STRUM AND PICK PATTERNS

This chart contains the suggested strum and pick patterns that are referred to by number at the beginning
of each song in this book. The symbols ⊓ and ∨ in the strum patterns refer to down and up strokes, respectively.
The letters in the pick patterns indicate which right-hand fingers play which strings.

p = thumb
i = index finger
m = middle finger
a = ring finger

For example; Pick Pattern 2
is played: thumb - index - middle - ring

Strum Patterns   ## Pick Patterns

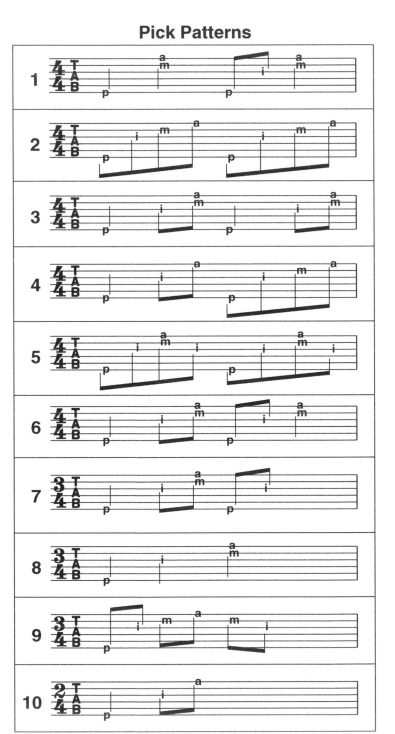

You can use the 3/4 Strum and Pick Patterns in songs written in compound meter (6/8, 9/8, 12/8, etc.).
For example, you can accompany a song in 6/8 by playing the 3/4 pattern twice in each measure.
The 4/4 Strum and Pick Patterns can be used for songs written in cut time (¢) by doubling the note
time values in the patterns. Each pattern would therefore last two measures in cut time.

CONTENTS

All I Want for Christmas Is My Two Front Teeth

Words and Music by Don Gardner

Strum Pattern: 3
Pick Pattern: 3

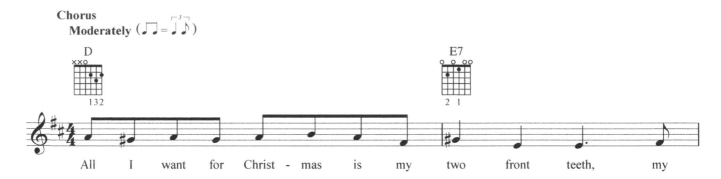

All I want for Christ-mas is my two front teeth, my

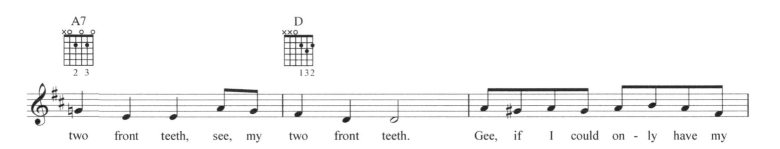

two front teeth, see, my two front teeth. Gee, if I could on-ly have my

two front teeth, then I could wish you, "Mer-ry Christ-mas!" 1. It

Verse

seems so long since I could say, "Sis-ter Su-zy sit-ting on a
2. *Spoken: Good ol' San-ta Claus and all his rein-deer; they used to bring me lots of toys and*

this-tle." Ev-'ry time I try to speak,
can-dy. Gee, but now when I go out and call, "Dan-cer, Pranc-er, Don-ner and Blitz-en,"

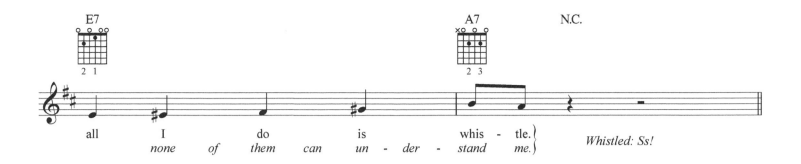

all I do is whis - tle.}
none of them can un - der - stand me.}
Whistled: Ss!

Outro-Chorus

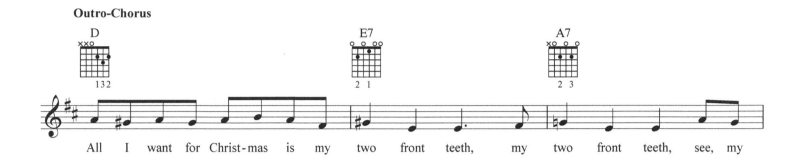

All I want for Christ-mas is my two front teeth, my two front teeth, see, my

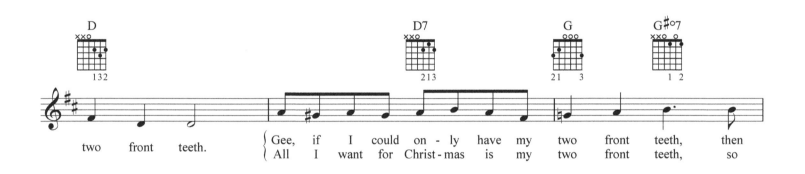

two front teeth. {Gee, if I could on - ly have my two front teeth, then
{All I want for Christ-mas is my two front teeth, so

1.

2. **Freely**

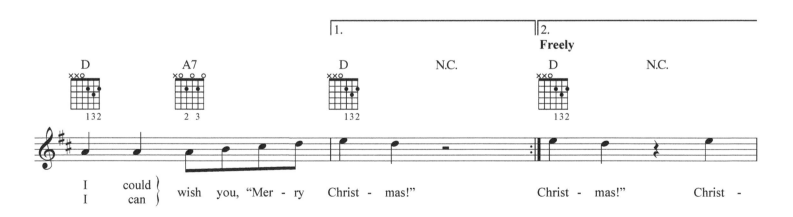

I could} I can} wish you, "Mer - ry Christ - mas!" Christ - mas!" Christ -

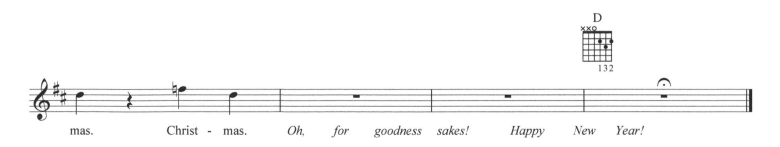

mas. Christ - mas. *Oh, for goodness sakes! Happy New Year!*

Caroling, Caroling

Words by Wihla Hutson
Music by Alfred Burt

Strum Pattern: 8
Pick Pattern: 8

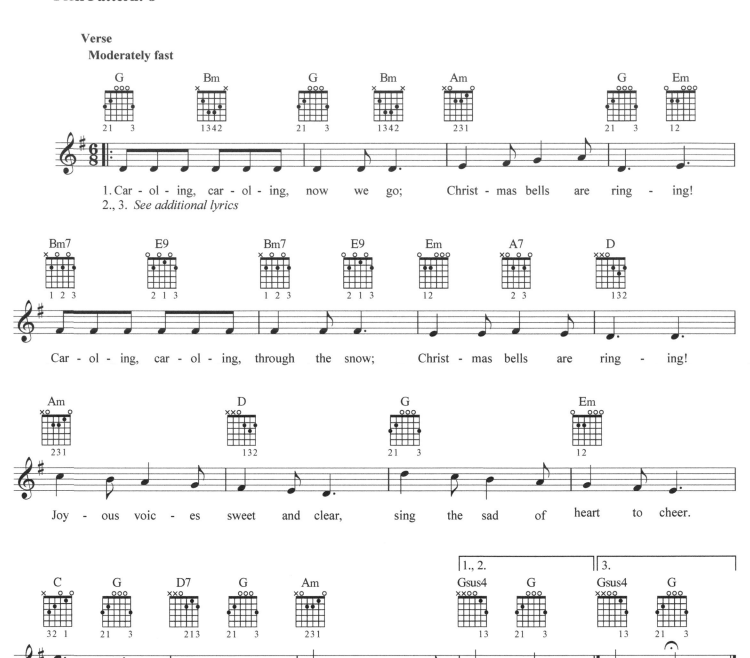

Additional Lyrics

2. Caroling, caroling, through the town;
   Christmas bells are ringing!
   Caroling, caroling, up and down;
   Christmas bells are ringing!
   Mark ye well the song we sing,
   Gladsome tidings now we bring.
   Ding, dong, ding, dong,
   Christmas bells are ringing!

3. Caroling, caroling, through the town;
   Christmas bells are ringing!
   Caroling, caroling, up and down;
   Christmas bells are ringing!
   Mark ye well the song we sing,
   Gladsome tidings now we bring.
   Ding, dong, ding, dong,
   Christmas bells are ringing!

Christmas Time Is Here

from A CHARLIE BROWN CHRISTMAS

Words by Lee Mendelson
Music by Vince Guaraldi

Strum Pattern: 7, 8
Pick Pattern: 8, 9

The Christmas Song
(Chestnuts Roasting on an Open Fire)

Music and Lyric by Mel Torme and Robert Wells

Strum Pattern: 2
Pick Pattern: 3

Verse
Moderately slow

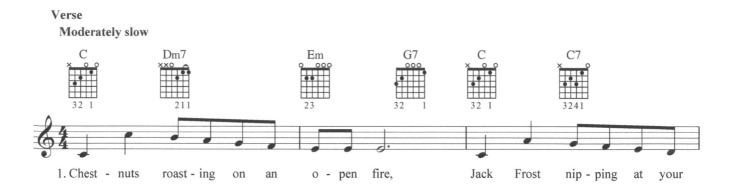

1. Chest - nuts roast - ing on an o - pen fire, Jack Frost nip - ping at your

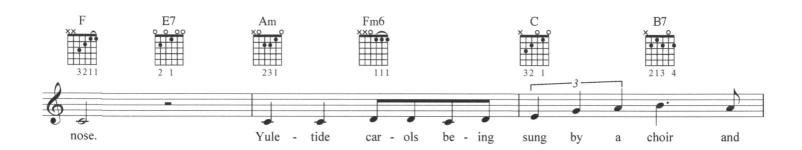

nose. Yule - tide car - ols be - ing sung by a choir and

Verse

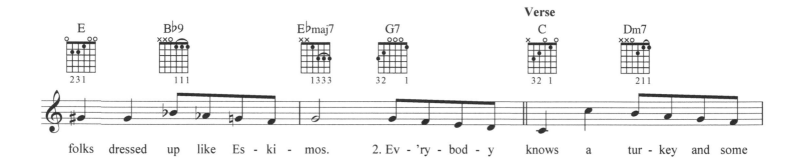

folks dressed up like Es - ki - mos. 2. Ev - 'ry - bod - y knows a tur - key and some

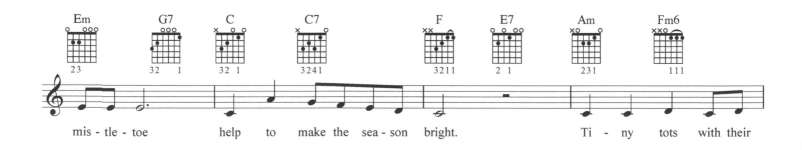

mis - tle - toe help to make the sea - son bright. Ti - ny tots with their

Do You Hear What I Hear

Words and Music by Noel Regney and Gloria Shayne

Strum Pattern: 4
Pick Pattern: 6

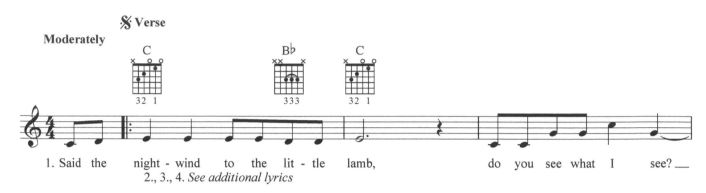

% Verse
Moderately

1. Said the night - wind to the lit - tle lamb, do you see what I see? ___
2., 3., 4. *See additional lyrics*

___ Way up in the sky, lit - tle lamb,

do you see what I see? _____ A star, a star,

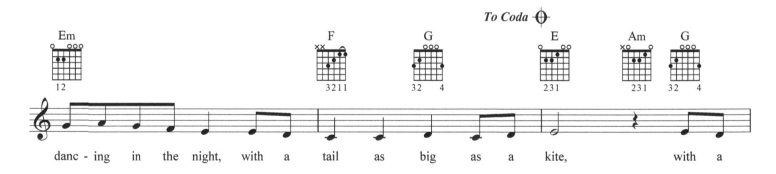

To Coda ⊕

danc - ing in the night, with a tail as big as a kite, with a

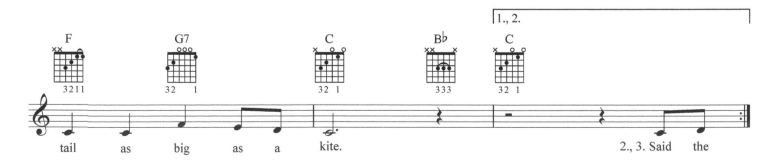

1., 2.

tail as big as a kite. 2., 3. Said the

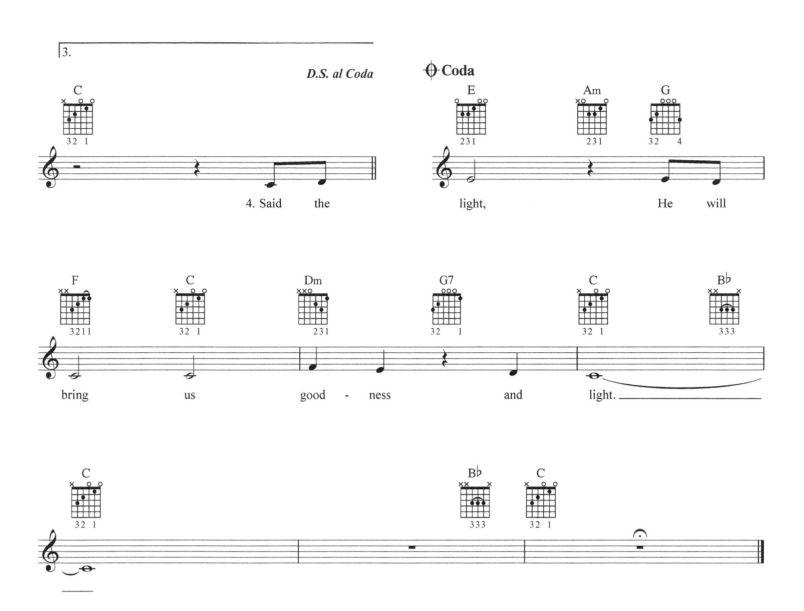

D.S. al Coda ⊕ **Coda**

C

4. Said the light, He will

F   C   Dm   G7   C   B♭

bring us good - ness and light.

C   B♭   C

Additional Lyrics

2. Said the little lamb to the shepherd boy,
   Do you hear what I hear?
   Ringing through the sky, shepherd boy,
   Do you hear what I hear?
   A song, a song, high above the tree,
   With a voice as big as the sea,
   With a voice as big as the sea.

3. Said the shepherd boy to the mighty king,
   Do you know what I know?
   In your palace warm, mighty king,
   Do you know what I know?
   A Child, a Child shivers in the cold,
   Let us bring him silver and gold,
   Let us bring him silver and gold.

4. Said the king to the people ev'rywhere,
   Listen to what I say!
   Pray for peace, people ev'rywhere,
   Listen to what I say!
   The Child, the Child, sleeping in the night;
   He will bring us goodness and light,
   He will bring us goodness and light.

Feliz Navidad

Music and Lyrics by José Feliciano

Strum Pattern: 2, 1
Pick Pattern: 4, 2

Happy Holiday

from the Motion Picture Irving Berlin's HOLIDAY INN
Words and Music by Irving Berlin

Strum Pattern: 3, 2
Pick Pattern: 3, 4

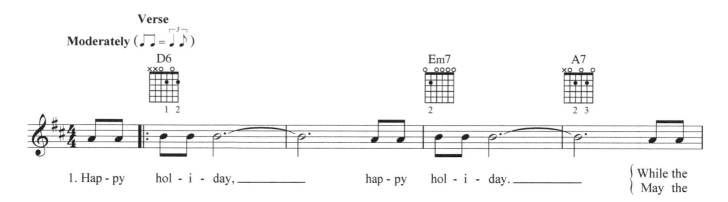

1. Hap - py hol - i - day,_____ hap - py hol - i - day._____ { While the / May the

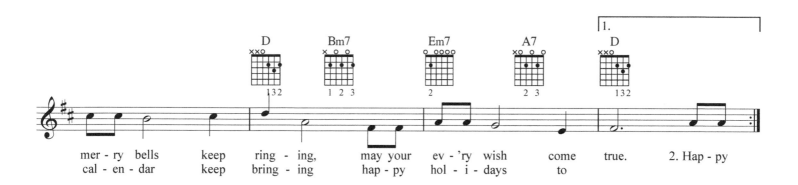

mer - ry bells keep ring - ing, may your ev - 'ry wish come true. 2. Hap - py
cal - en - dar keep bring - ing hap - py hol - i - days to

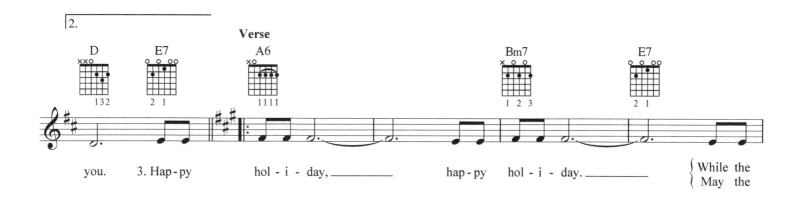

you. 3. Hap - py hol - i - day,_____ hap - py hol - i - day._____ { While the / May the

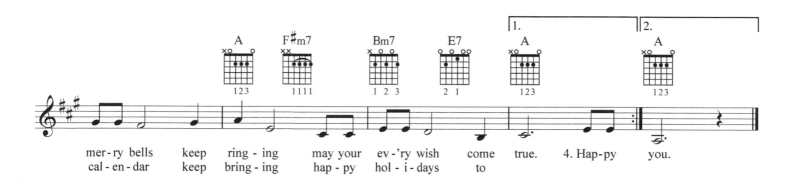

mer - ry bells keep ring - ing may your ev - 'ry wish come true. 4. Hap - py you.
cal - en - dar keep bring - ing hap - py hol - i - days to

Frosty the Snow Man

Words and Music by Steve Nelson and Jack Rollins

Strum Pattern: 3, 2
Pick Pattern: 3, 4

Verse
Moderately fast

1. Frost - y the snow man was a jol - ly hap - py soul, with a
3. Frost - y the snow man knew the sun was hot that day, so he

corn cob pipe and a but - ton nose ans two eyes made out of coal.
said, "Let's run and we'll have some fun now be - fore I melt a - way."

Frost - y the snow man is a fair - y tale they say. He was
Down to the vil - lage with a broom - stick in his hand, run - ning

made of snow but the chil - dren know how he came to life one day. There
here and there all a - round the square, say - in', "Catch me if you can." He

Happy Xmas
(War Is Over)
Written by John Lennon and Yoko Ono

Strum Pattern: 8
Pick Pattern: 8

1. So this is (3.) Christmas and what have {you}{we} done? An-oth-er year

o-ver, and a new one just be-gun. ___ And so {this is}{hap-py} Christ-mas, {I}{we} hope you have

fun, the near and the dear ones, the old and the young. ___ A mer-ry, mer-ry

To Coda ⊕

Christ-mas ___ and a hap-py new year, let's hope it's a good one ___ with-out an-y

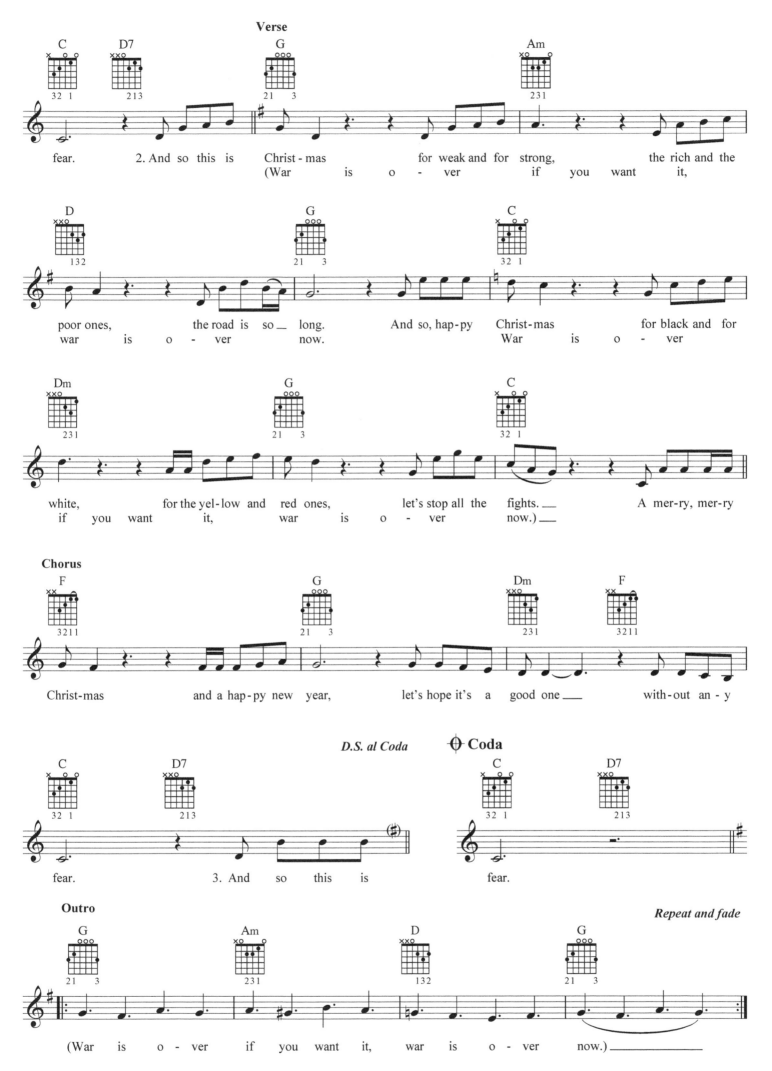

Have Yourself a Merry Little Christmas

from MEET ME IN ST. LOUIS

Words and Music by Hugh Martin and Ralph Blane

Strum Pattern: 4
Pick Pattern: 4

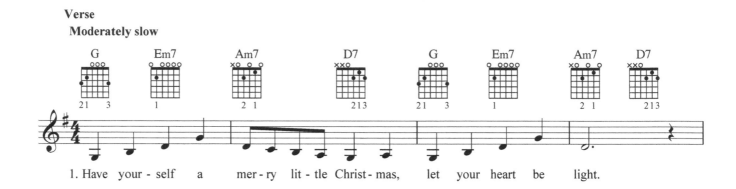

Verse
Moderately slow

1. Have your-self a mer-ry lit-tle Christ-mas, let your heart be light.

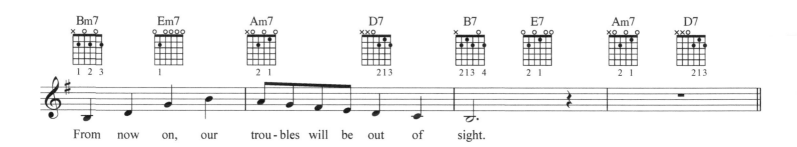

From now on, our trou-bles will be out of sight.

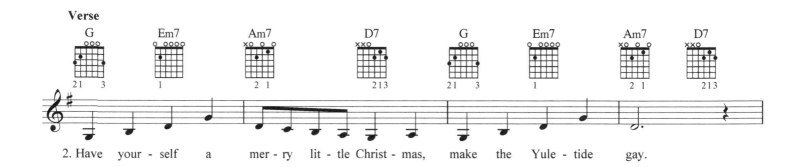

Verse

2. Have your-self a mer-ry lit-tle Christ-mas, make the Yule-tide gay.

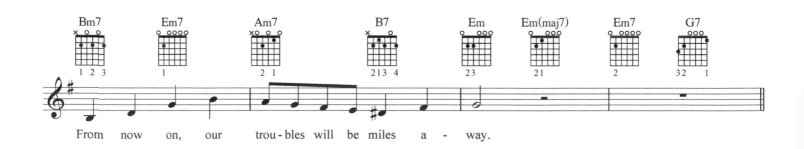

From now on, our trou-bles will be miles a - way.

Bridge

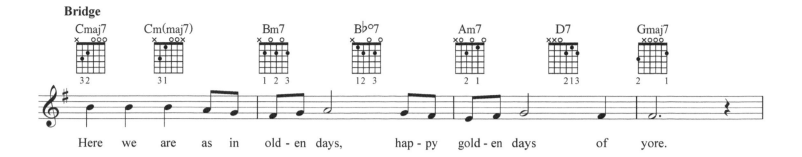

Here we are as in old-en days, hap-py gold-en days of yore.

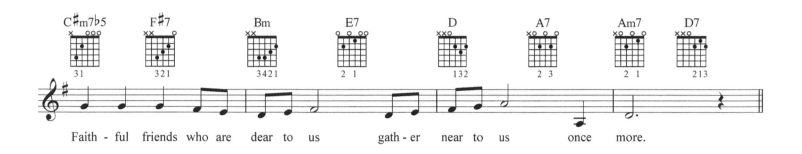

Faith-ful friends who are dear to us gath-er near to us once more.

Outro-Verse

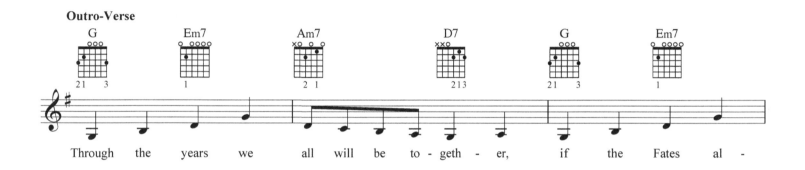

Through the years we all will be to-geth-er, if the Fates al-

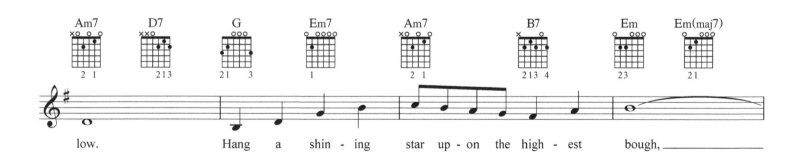

low. Hang a shin-ing star up-on the high-est bough, _____

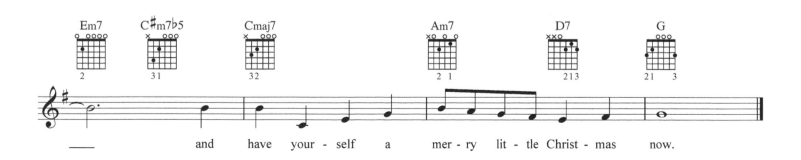

_____ and have your-self a mer-ry lit-tle Christ-mas now.

Here Comes Santa Claus
(Right Down Santa Claus Lane)

Words and Music by Gene Autry and Oakley Haldeman

Strum Pattern: 4
Pick Pattern: 1

Additional Lyrics

2. Here comes Santa Claus! Here comes Santa Claus!
   Right down Santa Claus Lane.
   He's got a bag that's filled with toys for the boys and girls again.
   Hear those sleigh bells jingle jangle, oh, what a beautiful sight.
   So jump in bed, and cover your head, 'cause Santa Claus comes tonight.

3. Here comes Santa Claus! Here comes Santa Claus!
   Right down Santa Claus Lane.
   He doesn't care if you're rich or poor, he loves you just the same.
   Santa knows we're all God's children, that makes ev'rything right.
   So fill your hearts with Christmas cheer, 'cause Santa Claus comes tonight.

4. Here comes Santa Claus! Here comes Santa Claus!
   Right down Santa Claus Lane.
   He'll come around when chimes ring out that it's Christmas morn again.
   Peace on earth will come to all if we just follow the light.
   So let's give thanks to the Lord above, 'cause Santa Claus comes tonight.

A Holly Jolly Christmas

Music and Lyrics by Johnny Marks

Strum Pattern: 2, 3
Pick Pattern: 3

(There's No Place Like)
Home for the Holidays

Words and Music by Al Stillman and Robert Allen

Strum Pattern: 3
Pick Pattern: 3

van - ia folks are trav - 'lin' down to Dix - ie's sun - ny shore; } From At -
for - nia to New Eng - land down to Dix - ie's sun - ny shore; }

lan - tic to Pa - ci - fic, gee, the traf - fic is ter - ri - fic. Oh, there's

Chorus

no place like home for the hol - i - days, _____ 'cause no mat - ter how

far a - way you roam, _____ if you want to be hap - py in a

mil - lion ways, _____ for the hol - i - days you can't beat home, sweet home. _____

_____ Oh, there's can't beat home, sweet home. _____

I Saw Mommy Kissing Santa Claus

Words and Music by Tommie Connor

Strum Pattern: 2, 3
Pick Pattern: 3, 4

I'll Be Home for Christmas

Words and Music by Kim Gannon and Walter Kent

Strum Pattern: 4, 3
Pick Pattern: 4, 3

It's Beginning to Look Like Christmas

By Meredith Willson

Strum Pattern: 2, 3
Pick Pattern: 3, 4

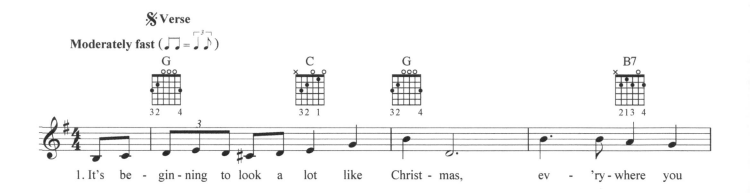

1. It's be - gin - ning to look a lot like Christ - mas, ev - 'ry - where you

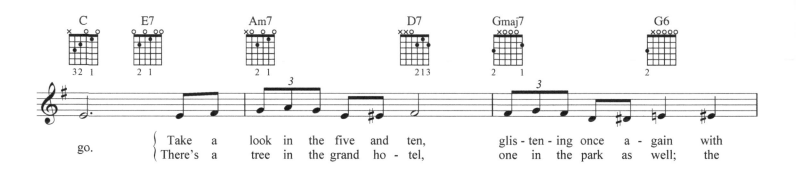

go.
{ Take a look in the five and ten,   glis - ten - ing once a - gain with
There's a tree in the grand ho - tel,   one in the park as well; the

can - dy canes and sil - ver lanes a - glow. }   It's be - gin - ning to look a lot like
stur - dy kind that does - n't mind the snow. }

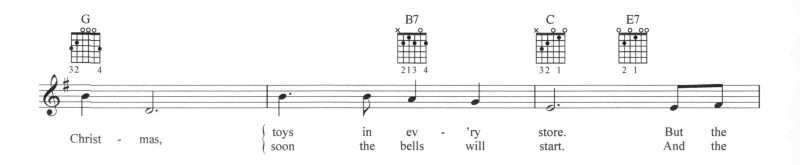

Christ - mas,
{ toys   in ev - 'ry   store.   But the
soon   the bells will   start.   And the

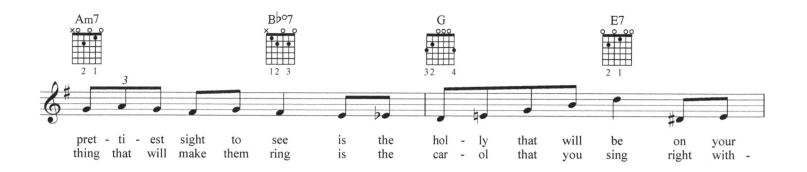

pret - ti - est sight to see   is   the   hol - ly   that   will   be   on   your

thing that will make them ring   is   the   car - ol   that   you   sing   right   with -

To Coda ⊕

Bridge

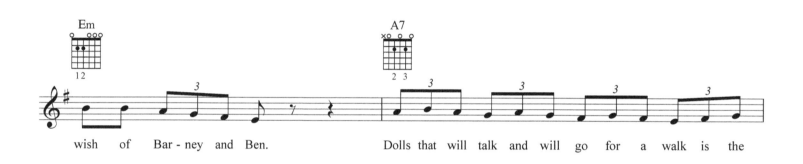

own   front   door.   A   pair   of   hop - a - long boots and   a   pis - tol that shoots is the

in   your

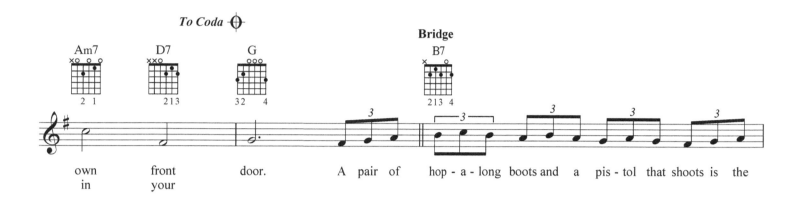

wish   of   Bar - ney   and   Ben.   Dolls   that   will   talk   and   will   go   for   a   walk   is   the

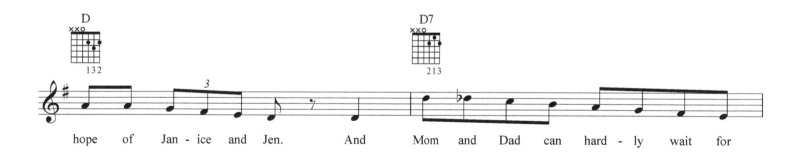

hope   of   Jan - ice   and   Jen.   And   Mom   and   Dad   can   hard - ly   wait   for

D.S. al Coda   ⊕ **Coda**

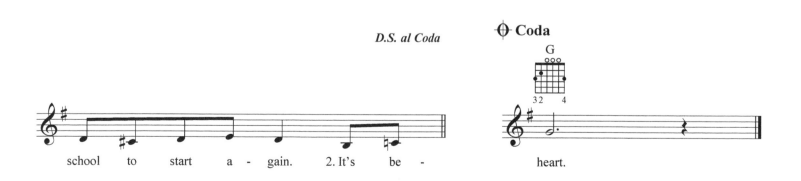

school   to   start   a - gain.   2. It's   be -   heart.

Jingle Bell Rock

Words and Music by Joe Beal and Jim Boothe

Strum Pattern: 1, 3
Pick Pattern: 2, 3

Bridge

C C7 F F#°7 C

air. What a bright time, it's the right time to rock the night a-

D7 G7

way. Jin-gle-bell time is a swell time to go gli-din' in a

Outro

C Cmaj7 C

one-horse sleigh. _ Gid-dy-ap, jin-gle horse pick up your feet,

A7 F

jin-gle a-round the clock. Mix and min-gle in a

Fm |1. D7 G7 C G7 ‖2. D7 G7

jin-gl-in' beat, that's the jin-gle-bell rock. that's the jin-gle-bell,

D7 G7 D7 G7 C

that's the jin-gle-bell, that's the jin-gle-bell rock. _____

Let It Snow! Let It Snow! Let It Snow!

Words by Sammy Cahn
Music by Jule Styne

Strum Pattern: 2
Pick Pattern: 4

The Little Drummer Boy

Words and Music by Harry Simeone, Henry Onorati and Katherine Davis

Strum Pattern: 3, 4
Pick Pattern: 1, 3

Little Saint Nick

Words and Music by Brian Wilson and Mike Love

Strum Pattern: 2
Pick Pattern: 4

Additional Lyrics

2. Just a little bobsled, we call it Old Saint Nick,
   But she'll walk a toboggan with a four-speed stick.
   She's candy-apple red with a ski for a wheel,
   And when Santa hits he gas, man just watch her peel.
   It's the Little Saint Nick. (Little Saint Nick.)
   It's the Little Saint Nick. (Little Saint Nick.)

3. And haulin' through the snow at fright'nin' speed
   With half a dozen deer with Rudy to lead.
   He's gotta wear his goggles 'cause the snow really flies,
   And he's cruisin' ev'ry pad with a little surprise.
   It's the Little Saint Nick. (Little Saint Nick.)
   It's the Little Saint Nick. (Little Saint Nick.)

Merry Christmas, Darling

Words and Music by Richard Carpenter and Frank Pooler

Strum Pattern: 4
Pick Pattern: 1

Greet - ing cards have all been sent, the Christ - mas rush is through,

but I still have one wish to make, a spe - cial one for you.

Mer - ry Christ - mas, dar - ling. We're a - part, that's true; but

I can dream and in my dreams, I'm Christ - mas - ing with you.

Hol - i - days are joy - ful, there's al - ways some - thing new. But

The Most Wonderful Time of the Year

Words and Music by Eddie Pola and George Wyle

Strum Pattern: 7
Pick Pattern: 8

My Favorite Things

from THE SOUND OF MUSIC
Lyrics by Oscar Hammerstein II
Music by Richard Rodgers

Strum Pattern: 8
Pick Pattern: 8

Additional Lyrics

2. Cream-colored ponies and crisp apple strudles,
   Doorbells and sleigh bells and schnitzel with noodles,
   Wild geese that fly with the moon on their wings,
   These are a few of my favorite things.

Pretty Paper

Words and Music by Willie Nelson

Strum Pattern: 8, 7
Pick Pattern: 8, 9

1. Crowd-ed streets, bus-y feet hus-tle by him. _____ Down-town shop-pers, Christ-mas is nigh. _____ There he sits all a-lone on the side-walk, _____ hop-ing that you won't pass him by. _____ 2. Should you stop; bet-ter not, much too bus-y. _____ You're in a hur-ry, my how time does

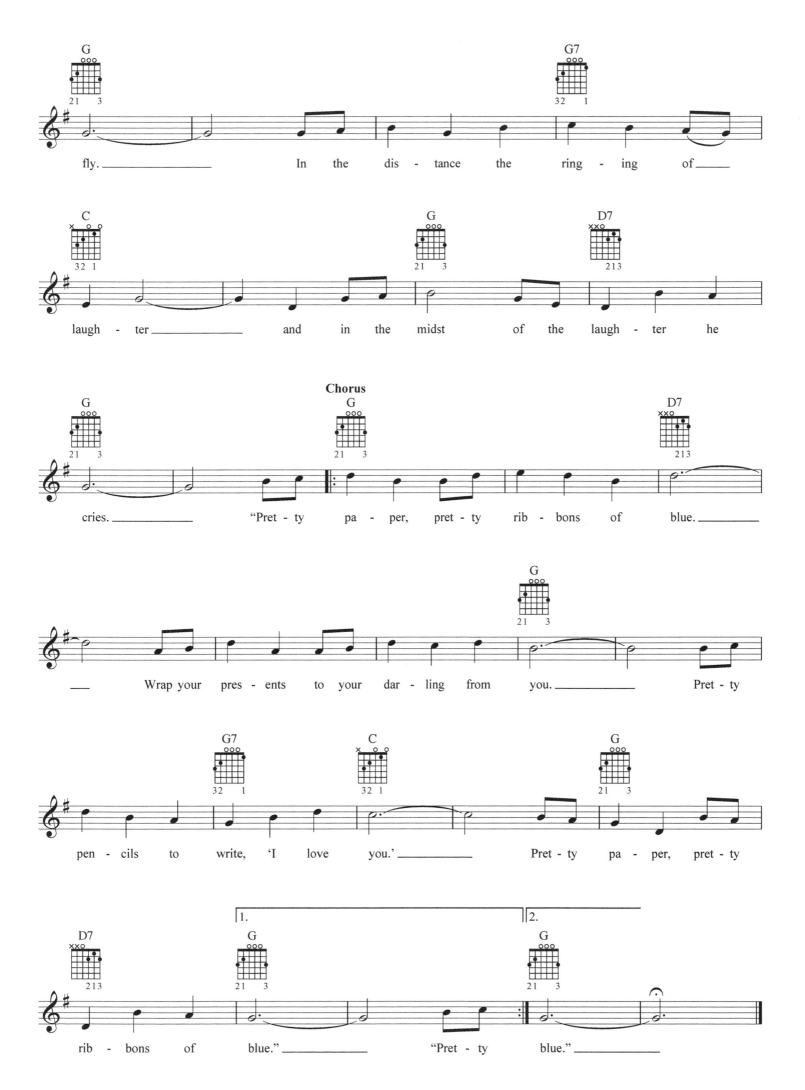

fly. _____ In the dis - tance the ring - ing of _____

laugh - ter _____ and in the midst of the laugh - ter he

Chorus

cries. _____ "Pret - ty pa - per, pret - ty rib - bons of blue. _____

_____ Wrap your pres - ents to your dar - ling from you. _____ Pret - ty

pen - cils to write, 'I love you.' _____ Pret - ty pa - per, pret - ty

1.

rib - bons of blue." _____ "Pret - ty

2.

blue." _____

Rudolph the Red-Nosed Reindeer

Music and Lyrics by Johnny Marks

Intro
Freely

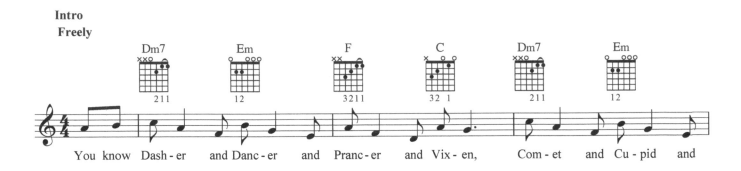

You know Dash-er and Danc-er and Pranc-er and Vix-en, Com-et and Cu-pid and

Don-ner and Blitz-en, but do you re-call the most fa-mous rein-deer of all?

Strum Pattern: 2, 3
Pick Pattern: 2, 3

Verse
Moderately

1., 2. Ru-dolph, the red-nosed rein-deer had a ver-y shin-y nose,

and if you ev-er saw it, you would e-ven say it glows.

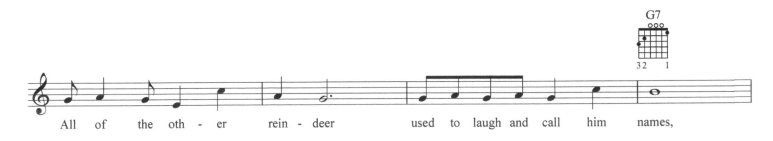

All of the oth-er rein-deer used to laugh and call him names,

Sleigh Ride

Music by Leroy Anderson

Strum Pattern: 3
Pick Pattern: 3

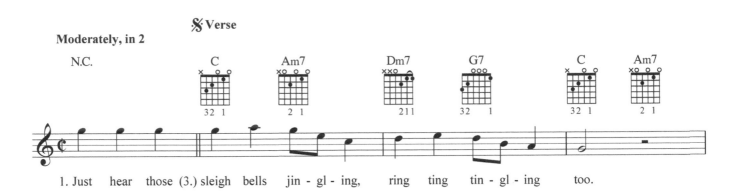

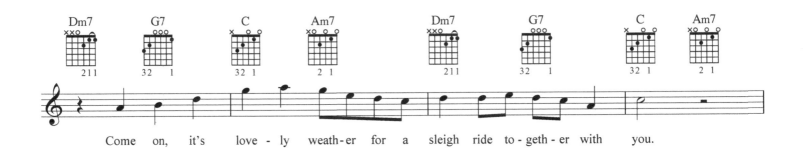

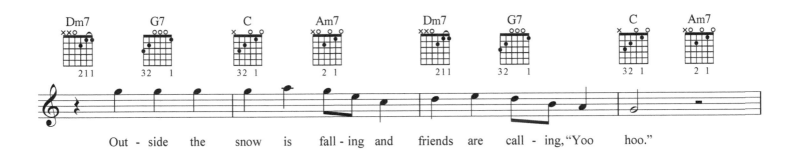

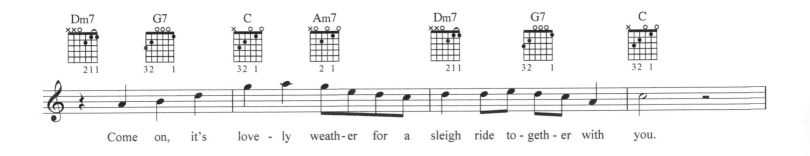

Bridge

Gid - dy - yap, gid - dy - yap, gid - dy - yap, let's go, let's look at the

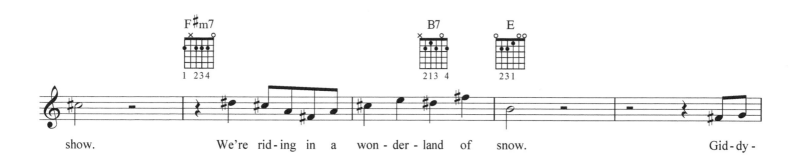

show. We're rid - ing in a won - der - land of snow. Gid - dy -

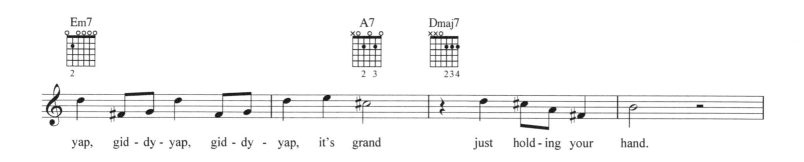

yap, gid - dy - yap, gid - dy - yap, it's grand just hold - ing your hand.

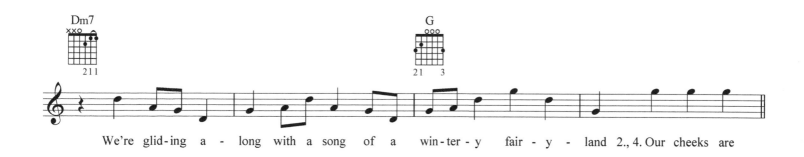

We're glid - ing a - long with a song of a win - ter - y fair - y - land 2., 4. Our cheeks are

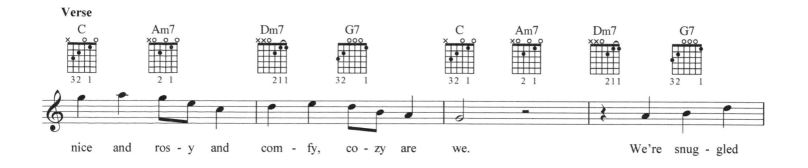

Verse

nice and ros - y and com - fy, co - zy are we. We're snug - gled

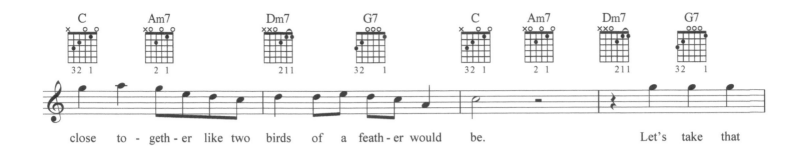

close to-geth-er like two birds of a feath-er would be. Let's take that

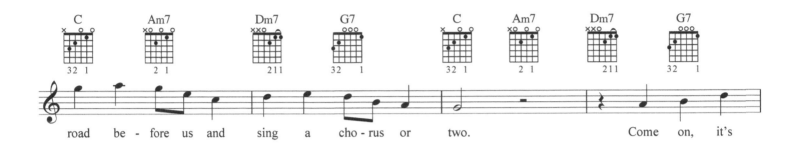

road be-fore us and sing a cho-rus or two. Come on, it's

To Coda ⊕

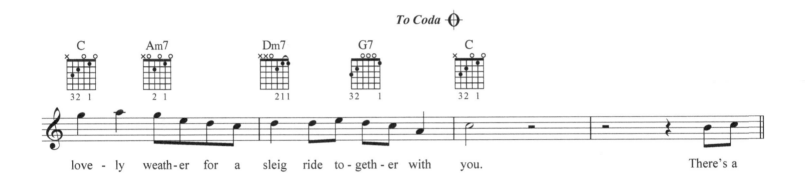

love-ly weath-er for a sleig ride to-geth-er with you. There's a

Bridge

birth - day par - ty at the home of farm - er Gray. It - 'll
hap - py feel - ing noth - ing in the world can buy when they

be the per - fect end - ing of a per - fect day. We'll be
pass a - round the cof - fee and the pump - kin pie. It - 'll

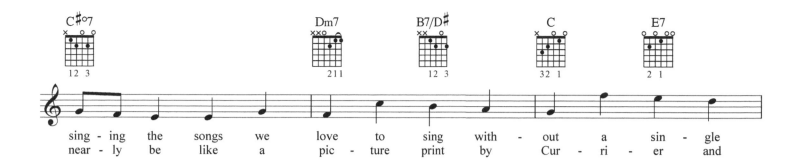

sing - ing the songs we love to sing with - out a sin - gle
near - ly be like a pic - ture print by Cur - ri - er and

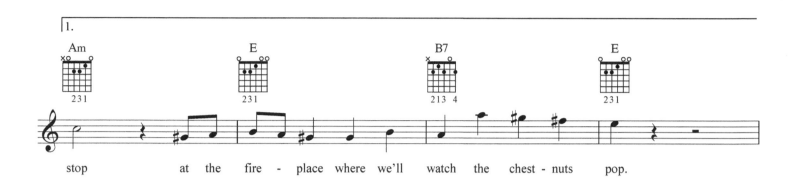

1.

stop   at the fire - place where we'll watch the chest - nuts pop.

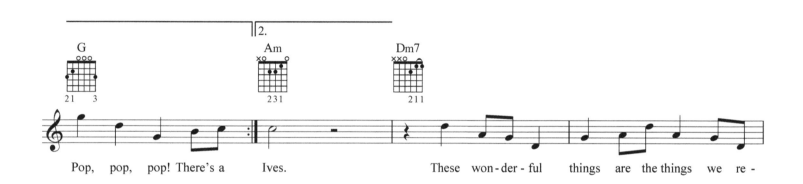

2.

Pop, pop, pop! There's a Ives.   These won - der - ful things are the things we re -

D.S. al Coda   ⊕ **Coda**

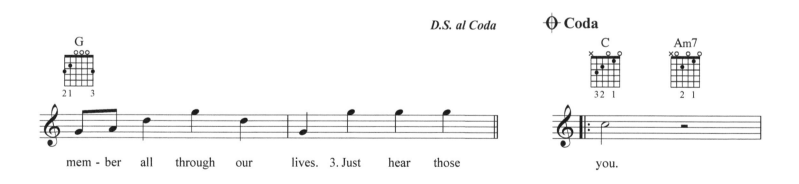

mem - ber all through our lives. 3. Just hear those   you.

Repeat & fade

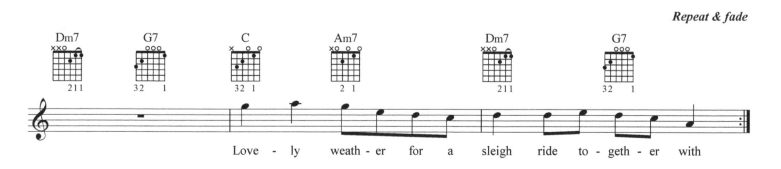

Love - ly weath - er for a sleigh ride to - geth - er with

This Christmas

Words and Music by Donny Hathaway and Nadine McKinnor

*Strum Pattern: 2
*Pick Pattern: 4

Intro
Moderately

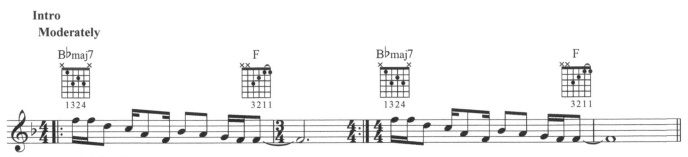

* Use Patterns 7 & 9 for 3/4 measures.

Verse

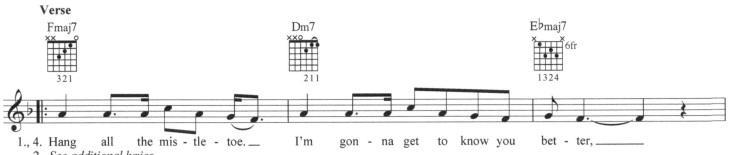

1., 4. Hang all the mis - tle - toe. __ I'm gon - na get to know you bet - ter, _____
2. *See additional lyrics*
3. *Instrumental*

this Christ - mas. And as we trim the tree, __ how much fun it's gon - na be to -

Chorus

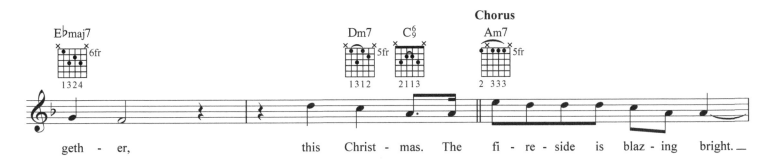

geth - er, this Christ - mas. The fi - re - side is blaz - ing bright. __

___ We're car - ol - in' through the night. _____ And this

Christ-mas will be a ver-y spe-cial Christ-mas _____ for _ me. _____

1., 2., 3.

4.

Mer-ry Christ-mas. _____

Shake your hand, shake your hand now. Wish your broth-er Mer-ry Christ-mas _

_____ all o-ver the land _____ now.

Outro

Repeat and fade

Additional Lyrics

2. Presents and cards are here.
   My world is filled with cheer and you,
   This Christmas.
   And as I look around,
   Your eyes outshine the town, they do,
   This Christmas.

Winter Wonderland

Words by Dick Smith
Music by Felix Bernard

Strum Pattern: 3, 4
Pick Pattern: 3, 4

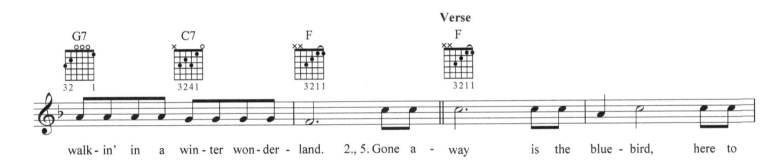

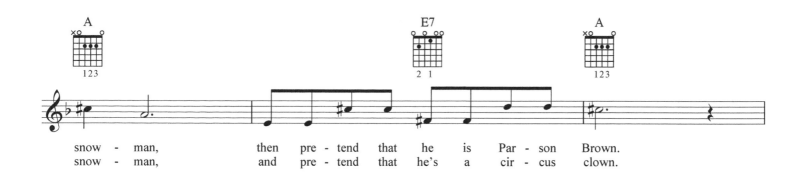

snow - man,   then pre- tend that he is Par - son Brown.
snow - man,   and pre- tend that he's a cir - cus clown.

He'll say, "Are you mar- ried?" We'll say, "No, man! But   you can do the job when you're in
We'll have lots of fun with Mis- ter Snow- man, un - til the oth- er kid - dies knock 'im

Verse

town!" 3. Lat - er on,   we'll con - spire, ___   as we dream   by the
down! 6. When it snows,   ain't it thrill - in',   tho' your nose   gets a

fire, _____   to face un - a - fraid, __   the plans that we made, __ }
chill - in'?   We'll frol - ic and play __   the Es - ki - mo way, __ }

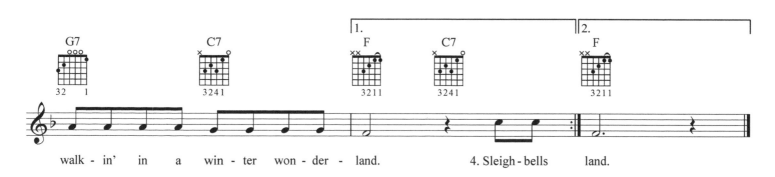

walk- in' in a win- ter won- der - land.   4. Sleigh- bells   land.

Wonderful Christmastime

Words and Music by Paul McCartney

Strum Pattern: 2
Pick Pattern: 4

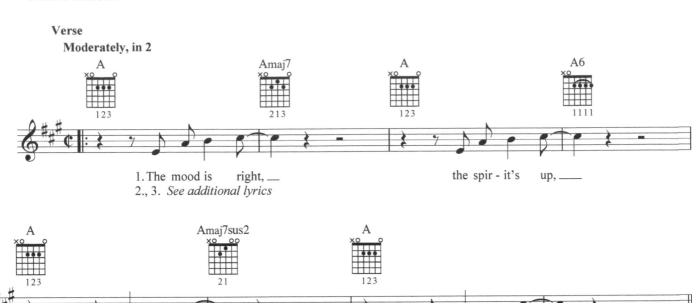

1. The mood is right, __ the spir - it's up, __
2., 3. *See additional lyrics*

we're here to - night __ and that's e - nough. __

Chorus

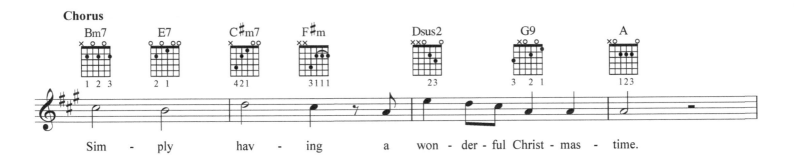

Sim - ply hav - ing a won - der - ful Christ - mas - time.

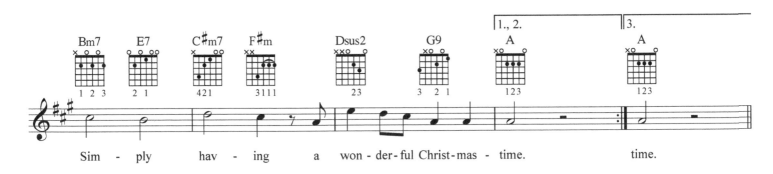

Sim - ply hav - ing a won - der - ful Christ - mas - time. time.

Bridge

To Coda ⊕

The choir of chil - dren sing their song. {(They prac - tised all year long.)} Ding dong, ding

Silver Bells

from the Paramount Picture THE LEMON DROP KID
Words and Music by Jay Livingston and Ray Evans

Strum Pattern: 9
Pick Pattern: 8

1. Cit-y side-walks, bus-y side-walks dressed in hol-i-day style, in the air there's a
2. *See additional lyrics*

feel-ing ___ of Christ-mas. ___ Chil-dren laugh-ing, peo-ple pass-ing, meet-ing smile af-ter

Chorus

smile, and on ev-'ry street cor-ner you hear: ___ Sil-ver bells, ___ sil-ver bells. ___

___ It's Christ-mas time in the cit-y. Ring-a-ling, ___ hear them ring. ___

1. ___ Soon it will be Christ-mas day.
2. 2. Strings of day. ___

Additional Lyrics

2. Strings of street lights, even stop lights
Blink a bright red and green,
As the shoppers rush home with their treasures.
Hear the snow crunch, see the kids bunch,
This is Santa's big scene,
And above all the bustle you hear:

Celebrate Christmas
WITH YOUR GUITAR AND HAL LEONARD

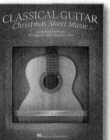

THE BEST CHRISTMAS GUITAR FAKE BOOK EVER
INCLUDES TAB

Over 150 Christmas classics for guitar. Songs include: Blue Christmas • The Chipmunk Song • Frosty the Snow Man • Happy Holiday • A Holly Jolly Christmas • I Saw Mommy Kissing Santa Claus • I Wonder As I Wander • Jingle-Bell Rock • Rudolph, the Red-Nosed Reindeer • Santa Bring My Baby Back (To Me) • Suzy Snowflake • Tennessee Christmas • and more.
00240053 Melody/Lyrics/Chords $25.00

THE BIG CHRISTMAS COLLECTION FOR EASY GUITAR

Includes over 70 Christmas favorites, such as: Ave Maria • Blue Christmas • Deck the Hall • Feliz Navidad • Frosty the Snow Man • Happy Holiday • A Holly Jolly Christmas • Joy to the World • O Holy Night • Silver and Gold • Suzy Snowflake • and more. Does not include TAB.
00698978 Easy Guitar $17.99

CHRISTMAS CAROLS
For Easy Guitar

24 holiday favorites, including: Carol of the Bells • Good King Wenceslas • Hark! the Herald Angels Sing • I Saw Three Ships • Jingle Bells • Jolly Old St. Nicholas • O Come, O Come Immanuel • O Little Town of Bethlehem • Up on the Housetop • and more. Does not include TAB.
00702221 Easy Guitar $10.99

CHRISTMAS CAROLS
Guitar Chord Songbook

80 favorite carols for guitarists who just need the lyrics and chords: Angels We Have Heard on High • Away in a Manger • Deck the Hall • Good King Wenceslas • The Holly and the Ivy • Irish Carol • Jingle Bells • Joy to the World • O Holy Night • Rocking • Silent Night • Up on the Housetop • Welsh Carol • What Child Is This? • and more.
00699536 Lyrics/Chord Symbols/
Guitar Chord Diagrams $14.99

CLASSICAL GUITAR CHRISTMAS SHEET MUSIC

30 top holiday songs: Away in a Manger • Deck the Hall • Go, Tell It on the Mountain • Hallelujah Chorus • I Saw Three Ships • Jingle Bells • O Little Town of Bethlehem • Silent Night • The Twelve Days of Christmas • Up on the Housetop • We Wish You a Merry Christmas • What Child Is This? • and more. Does not include TAB.
00146974 Solo Classical Guitar $10.99

CHRISTMAS JAZZ
Jazz Guitar Chord Melody Solos
INCLUDES TAB

21 songs in chord-melody style for the beginning to intermediate jazz guitarist in standard notation and tablature: Auld Lang Syne • Baby, It's Cold Outside • Cool Yule • Have Yourself a Merry Little Christmas • Mary, Did You Know? • Santa Baby • White Christmas • Winter Wonderland • and more.
00171334 Solo Guitar............................$15.99

CHRISTMAS SONGS FOR EASY GUITAR

20 classic Christmas tunes: Blue Christmas • The Christmas Song (Chestnuts Roasting) • Frosty the Snow Man • Christmas Time Is Here • A Holly Jolly Christmas • I Saw Mommy Kissing Santa Claus • I'll Be Home for Christmas • Jingle-Bell Rock • Merry Christmas, Darling • Rudolph the Red-Nosed Reindeer • Silver Bells • You're All I Want for Christmas • and more.
00699804 Easy Guitar $7.99

FINGERPICKING CHRISTMAS SONGS
INCLUDES TAB

15 songs for intermediate-level guitarists, combining melody and harmony in superb fingerpicking arrangements: Baby, It's Cold Outside • Caroling, Caroling • Have Yourself a Merry Little Christmas • I Heard the Bells on Christmas Day • The Little Drummer Boy • Mary, Did You Know? • Mele Kalikimaka • Sleigh Ride • White Christmas • Wonderful Christmastime • and more.
00171333 Fingerstyle Guitar $10.99

FINGERPICKING YULETIDE
INCLUDES TAB

Carefully written for intermediate-level guitarists, this collection includes an introduction to fingerstyle guitar and 16 holiday favorites: Do You Hear What I Hear • Happy Xmas (War Is Over) • A Holly Jolly Christmas • Jingle-Bell Rock • Rudolph the Red-Nosed Reindeer • and more.
00699654 Fingerstyle Guitar $12.99

FIRST 50 CHRISTMAS CAROLS YOU SHOULD PLAY ON GUITAR
INCLUDES TAB

Accessible, must-know Christmas songs are included in this collection arranged for guitar solo with a combo of tab, chords and lyrics. Includes: Angels We Have Heard on High • The First Noel • God Rest Ye Merry, Gentlemen • The Holly and the Ivy • O Christmas Tree • Silent Night • Up on the Housetop • What Child Is This? • and more.
00236224 Guitar Solo...........................$12.99

3-CHORD CHRISTMAS

You only need to know how to play 3 chords (G, C and D) on guitar to master these 25 holiday favorites: Away in a Manger • The Chipmunk Song • Frosty the Snow Man • Go, Tell It on the Mountain • Here Comes Santa Claus • Jingle Bells • The Little Drummer Boy • O Christmas Tree • Silent Night • Silver Bells • While Shepherds Watched Their Flocks • and more.
00146973 Guitar Solo...........................$10.99

THE ULTIMATE GUITAR CHRISTMAS FAKE BOOK
INCLUDES TAB

200 Christmas standards: All I Want for Christmas Is You • Baby, It's Cold Outside • The Christmas Song (Chestnuts Roasting on an Open Fire) • Do You Want to Build a Snowman? • Feliz Navidad • Frosty the Snow Man • A Holly Jolly Christmas • Jingle Bells • Let It Snow! Let It Snow! Let It Snow! • Mary, Did You Know? • Rockin' Around the Christmas Tree • Santa Baby • Silent Night • What Child Is This? • White Christmas • and more.
00236446 Melody/Lyrics/Chords $22.50

HAL•LEONARD®

www.halleonard.com

Prices, contents and availability subject to change without notice.

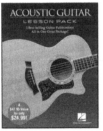

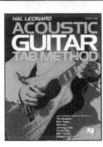